This Book Belongs To:

_____

Shaoey and Dot

Bug Meets Bundle

by **Mary Beth &**
Steven Curtis Chapman

Illustrated by Jim Chapman

www.tommynelson.com

A Division of Thomas Nelson, Inc.
www.ThomasNelson.com

Published in Nashville, Tennessee, by Tommy Nelson®, a Division of Thomas Nelson, Inc.

Library of Congress Cataloging-in-Publication Data
Chapman, Mary Beth.
  Shaoey and Dot : bug meets bundle / by Mary Beth and Steven Curtis
Chapman ; illustrated by Jim Chapman.
      p. cm.
  Summary: An abandoned Chinese baby who has been befriended by a
ladybug finds her way to an orphanage where she is eventually adopted by
an American family.
  ISBN 1-4003-0482-2 (hardcover)
  ISBN 1-4003-0553-5 (hardcover with dvd)
  [1. Intercountry adoption—Fiction. 2. Adoption—Fiction. 3.
China—Fiction. 4. Ladybugs—Fiction. 5. Stories in rhyme.] I. Chapman,
Steven Curtis. II. Chapman, Jim, 1956- ill. III. Title.
  PZ8.3.C3725Sh 2004
  [E]--dc22
                            2004011733

04 05 06 07 08 LBM 5 4 3 2 1
Printed in the United States of America

Dear Families,

For almost two years, our daughter Emily campaigned for us to adopt a baby girl. At first, we resisted the idea, but after spending a lot of time thinking and praying, as crazy as we thought it was, we were inspired to extend our family through the miracle of adoption. On March 16, 2000, we walked out of a hotel room in Changsha, Hunan, China, with our daughter Shaohannah (Shaoey, pronounced SHOW-ee, for short), and our lives were changed forever. Then, a little over two years later, at the dedication ceremony of our friend's adopted son from China, God spoke to us about adopting again. Within days we began the adoption process and went on to complete the adoption of our 7-month-old daughter Stevey Joy Ru Chapman in May of 2003.

Adoption is a perfect picture of what God has done for each of us in making us His children through Christ. Psalm 68:5–6 tells us that as the Father to the fatherless, God delights in setting the lonely in families. It has been our experience that the scriptural mandate of caring for orphans, such as the one found in James 1:27, is really a wonderful invitation to experience God in a profound way by being a part of His sovereign plan for His precious children.

Working from these foundational truths, we also founded Shaohannah's Hope, which exists to enable children living without the love and hope of an earthly family to be adopted into "covenant homes." These families can provide not only the love and support needed for this life, but also provide a child with the knowledge of God's plan for his or her eternal life with a forever family called The Body of Christ.

Steven Curtis Chapman
Mary Beth Chapman
Steven Curtis Chapman
Mary Beth Chapman
Co-Founders of Shaohannah's Hope
www.shaohannahshope.org

The day started out just like all days before,
With the sun peeking over the trees.
Dot let out a yawn as she stretched out her wings
And went out for a ride on the breeze.

She stopped on a leaf for a quick bite of breakfast
And sipped on a sweet drop of dew,
When off in the distance she heard a strange sound
That was different from any she knew.

Now being the curious bug that she was,
She had to go investigate,
So she followed the sound right down to the ground,
Where a bundle of rags had been placed.

Dot landed softly on top of the bundle.
Then all of a sudden, it wiggled!
She started to fly, then she peeked down inside
And saw something that caused her to giggle!

She carefully climbed her way down to a spot,
Right between two almond-shaped eyes.
"How cute is this?!" she said to herself.
"What a fabulous little surprise!"

Dot was so taken with this little creature
That she never heard footsteps approaching.
Suddenly, she was scooped up with the bundle,
Who was now causing quite a commotion.

The next thing she knew they were bumping along
In an old wooden basket on wheels.
Dot was afraid so she hid in a wrinkle
And did all she could not to squeal!

When they finally stopped moving, Dot slowly crawled out
To try and make an escape.
She started to fly, then the little thing cried,
As if saying, "Please don't go away!"

They were in a small room with one little window
That opened to Dot's world outside,
But she just couldn't leave her new little friend,
So she whispered, "I'll stay right by your side."

And so it was there in that moment of truth
That Dot's lifetime promise was heard
'Cause if you know anything about ladybugs,
You know they always keep their word.

Having made her decision to stay with her friend,
Dot said, "Wait here, while I go explore."
That's when she discovered the whole room was covered
With bunches of bundles galore.

There must've been dozens of almond-shaped eyes
All watching as she flew around.
Suddenly, Dot realized where they were—
"This is where babies come to be found!"

It was all making sense now! Each bed in the room
Held a lost little bundle of love,
And the sound they were making is the song babies sing
When they're needing their mothers to come.

Dot landed on top of her little friend's rear
And whispered, "I've got some great news!
We are where mommies and daddies come looking
To find special babies like you!
    (And special ladybugs like me too!)"

The waiting began, as the days turned to weeks;
Then one morning, Dot woke to the sound
Of the ladies in white who took care of the babies
All hustling and bustling around.

The next thing Dot knew, they were covered in bubbles,
Getting scrubbed from antennae to toe.
The ladies were saying, "Your family is waiting.
We'll miss you, but it's your turn to go."

On their way to the place where the family was waiting
Dot thought she should try to explain.
"Well, this is the day," she said to her friend.
"Everything's getting ready to change.

"See, I've waited till now to tell you this story.
It's about all the reasons you cry.
Sometimes it's because you feel sick, tired, or hungry,
And sometimes you just want your pants dry."

"But, then, there's a cry that's the saddest of all.
In fact, it's unlike any other.
It comes from a deep, empty place in your heart
That can only be filled by a mother.

"And after today, I will never again
Hear that sad song coming from you.
You're getting adopted, you're getting a mother,
And you're getting a family too!
    (Of course, I'll be right there with you. . . .
    We'll go to the park and the zoo
    And do all the things families do!)"

Dot was so caught up in telling her story
That she didn't realize what had happened.
When she looked up, she saw they were all in a room
With ten tearful eyes looking at them.

The cameras all flashed, and everywhere Dot looked,
She saw spots like the ones on her wings.
But what her ears heard was the prettiest song
That she'd ever heard anyone sing!

The mother was holding her new little one,
As her big tears came falling like rain.
Then even Dot's ladybug eyes started leaking
When she realized the song was a name.

She had wondered so long what her friend would be called,
And this name was so perfect and clever.
"From now on, we will be Shaoey and Dot,
And we'll be together forever!"

Everything was so strange and exciting and new,
And soon, they were ready to go.
They got in a thing with two humongous wings
That would take them to a place they'd call home!